Little Moreton Hall

Cheshire

THE NATIONAL TRUST

Introduction

The close oblique view from the Newcastle–Congleton road of the absurd half-timbered structure, crowned by an unbroken length of gallery window like some fantastic, elongated Chinese lantern, and toppling, if not positively bending over the tranquil water of a moat, the whole an ancient pack of cards about to meet from the first puff of wind its own reflection, is something which once seen can never be forgotten.

James Lees-Milne, *People and Places*

LITTLE MORETON HALL is perhaps the best-known example of timber-framed architecture in England. The Moretons had been powerful local landlords since the thirteenth century and had greatly increased the size of their estate by buying up land thrown on to the market following depopulation after the Black Death of 1348, and the Dissolution of the Monasteries from the 1530s to the 1550s.

The Great Hall and the northern half of the east range (see plan pp. 4–5) are probably the earliest surviving parts of Little Moreton. They date from the time of William Moreton I, in the early years of the sixteenth century. The east range was extended south shortly afterwards and the north-west wing and porch were added in about 1546. In 1559 a carpenter called Richard Dale carried out extensive work – including the two great bay windows in the courtyard for William Moreton II, who, shortly before his death in 1563, commenced the south range. His son John had the Parlour and Chapel painted, and the great long table and the octagonal table installed in the house.

Rising to three storeys, which include the famous Long Gallery, the south range contrasts with the strong and sturdy west wing of the 1540s in being more lightly framed and structurally adventurous. The range includes a hall and parlour for guests on the first floor and access is gained by a central newel staircase, which was installed late in the building programme, as confirmed by tree-ring analysis. The 68-feet-long Gallery was probably also something of an afterthought, but both it and the staircase were part of an uninterrupted sequence of construction.

The last extension at Little Moreton was a bake and brew-house with servants' quarters above, built on to the south range in the early seventeenth century. After this the house ceased to grow, largely because the Moretons paid a heavy price for choosing to be staunch Royalists in the Civil War. From the early eighteenth century, the family ceased to live at Little Moreton, which was let to tenant farmers for a further 200 years. At the end of the nineteenth century Elizabeth Moreton carried out much-needed restoration, which was continued by her cousin, Bishop Abraham, who succeeded to the house in 1912. Further substantial repairs to the ancient timbers have been necessary in recent years. It was through the generosity of the Bishop and his son, Rupert Abraham, that the hall passed to the National Trust in 1938. In five centuries it has never been sold.

Only three items of an inventory taken in 1654 on the death of William Moreton III have survived. None the less, the comparative emptiness of the interior provides an opportunity to appreciate the structural ingenuity of the Tudor craftsmen, whose carpentry, plasterwork, painting and glazing are all of the highest quality.

(Opposite) The gabled kitchen wing and Great Hall porch; engraving by Thomas Tagg after J. S. Cotman, from Britton's 'Architectural Antiquities of Great Britain' (1835)

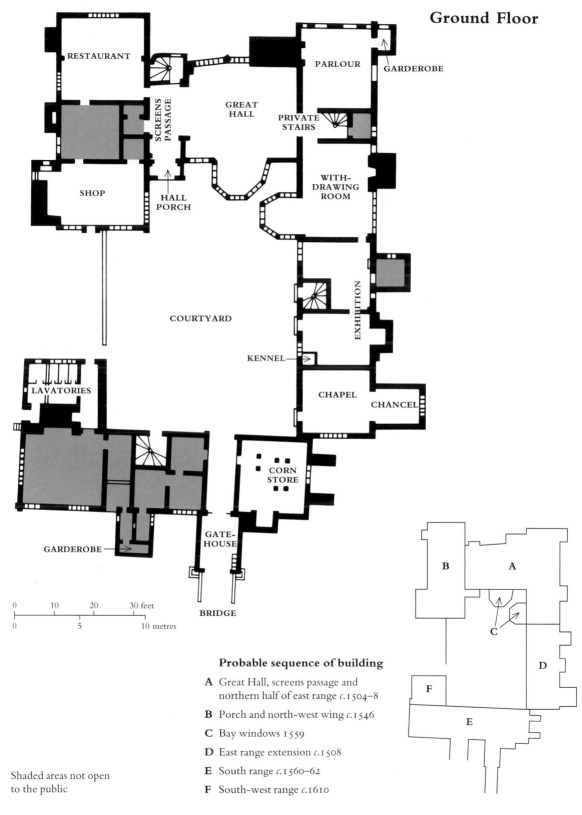

Ground Floor

RESTAURANT

PARLOUR

GARDEROBE

SCREENS PASSAGE

GREAT HALL

PRIVATE STAIRS

WITH-DRAWING ROOM

SHOP

HALL PORCH

COURTYARD

EXHIBITION

KENNEL

LAVATORIES

CHAPEL

CHANCEL

CORN STORE

GARDEROBE

GATE-HOUSE

| 0 | 10 | 20 | 30 feet |
| 0 | | 5 | 10 metres |

BRIDGE

Probable sequence of building

A Great Hall, screens passage and northern half of east range *c.*1504–8

B Porch and north-west wing *c.*1546

C Bay windows 1559

D East range extension *c.*1508

E South range *c.*1560–62

F South-west range *c.*1610

B A

C

F

D

E

Shaded areas not open to the public

First Floor

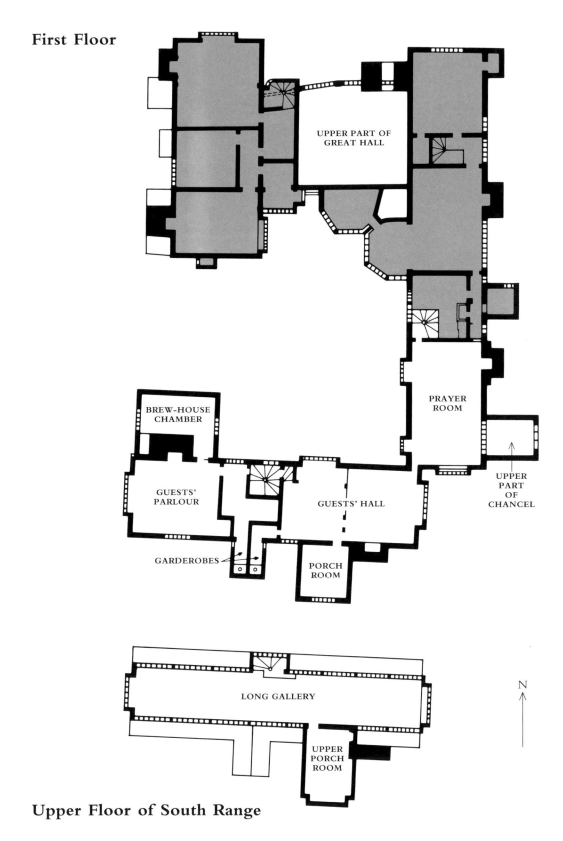

UPPER PART OF
GREAT HALL

BREW-HOUSE
CHAMBER

PRAYER
ROOM

GUESTS'
PARLOUR

GUESTS' HALL

UPPER
PART
OF
CHANCEL

GARDEROBES

PORCH
ROOM

LONG GALLERY

N

UPPER
PORCH
ROOM

Upper Floor of South Range

Tour of the House

The Exterior

One of the principal delights of Little Moreton Hall is that its timbers are arranged in a rich variety of patterns largely within square panels. Both square panelling and ornamental panelling of decorative timber framing, which were especially popular in Elizabethan times, are mainly found in the West Midlands and the Welsh borders. But it was the gentry of Lancashire and Cheshire who used these techniques to their most glorious and dazzling effect. Another local technique is that of coving – a concave plaster cove beneath each overhang or jetty.

The Gatehouse and South Range

Visitors enter Little Moreton through the Gatehouse in the south range, which was built in the early 1560s. Although the gatehouse displays such ancient motifs as interweaving vines, cable mouldings and trefoils, it also shows some attempt to copy the latest styles imported from the Italian Renaissance, in particular the 'anticke work' over the outer door and the friezes of masks to either side of the inner door. These carvings are very crude, and this is nowhere more apparent than in the ungainly warriors which, like those at Paycocke's in Coggeshall, Essex, stand sentinel on either side of the entrance to the Gatehouse.

The roof of the Gallery, which runs the length of the upper floor of the south range, is covered with immensely heavy gritstone slates, which may have come from Tegg's Mill quarry, two miles east of Macclesfield. Their weight has caused the structure beneath to settle gradually over the centuries.

The Courtyard

The porch in the corner of the courtyard and the adjoining north-west cross wing of *c.*1546 combine decorative framing with other motifs. Quatrefoils (resembling four-leaf clovers) have been carved out of solid wood in a style peculiar to this region. The mouldings and decorations of the porch and adjoining portion of the north-west wing are wholly late Gothic, with twisted columns and chamfered pilasters topped by plain capitals typical of the Perpendicular style.

The two-storey bay windows in the north-east corner were built by the carpenter Richard Dale in 1559, as the carved inscriptions announce. Dale was probably also responsible for the windows in the north-west wing opposite.

To the right is the east range extension, which was built around 1508, very shortly after the Great Hall, to provide further accommodation, together with a Chapel and Prayer Room. On the right is an original early sixteenth-century window with an interesting foliage frieze, and, on the left, a window which was probably built by Richard Dale in 1559; the latter replaced an earlier mullioned window, the mortice holes for which are visible in the Prayer Room.

The Garden Fronts

Move out of the courtyard and around the north-west wing, which has two huge brick kitchen chimneystacks on this side. Brick was scarce in Cheshire until the seventeenth century. With offset and corrugated upper flues, step bands and diamond-patterned faces, it is here used to best effect. While detail has been lost to nineteenth-century rebuilding, this 'diaper' work in blue headers can still be seen on the garden side of three of Little Moreton's seven stacks. Between the stacks on this side is a pair of first-floor doorways, which formerly gave access to a garderobe tower not unlike the two which survive on the east side of the east range. In 1991 that on the right was unbricked and a new oak plank door was fitted.

From the north, the view is of the other side of the 'H' plan of the early sixteenth-century house (A and B on the plan, see pp. 4–5). The

The Gatehouse and south range

Great Hall wall, recessed between flanking wings, is of plain post and studwork. The windows were put in by Richard Dale in 1559, when a first floor was inserted into the Great Hall. The wings, whose gables with their decorated corner posts face the Knot Garden, are distinguished by their riotous use of diagonal braces.

Glass

Thirty thousand leaded panes, known as quarries, pattern Little Moreton's windows. Complementing the exquisitely moulded timbers in which they are set, each group of lights is designed with a different arrangement of triangles, rectangles, diamonds, circles, squares and lozenges. *A Booke of Sundry Draughts, principally serving for glaziers*, published in 1615, contains over a hundred designs for lead glazing. Whilst there have been losses, there is still some ancient mouth-blown glass at Little Moreton. Modern float glass, being perfect, is flat in appearance whereas spun crown and cylinder-made glass is fiery or iridescent and, being unbleached, often tinted by trace impurities of copper, iron, and manganese.

By 1589 there were fifteen glass factories in England, the nearest being at Bishop's Wood, Eccleshall and on Cannock Chase in Stafford-

shire. Archaeological excavation has recently identified a glass site near Biddulph Old Hall, just four miles away, and it is possible that itinerant smiths travelled to the area to supply Richard Dale's fenestrations around 1560. Being thin and uneven, such glass is too fragile to be cut with a diamond point, so was cleaved into quarries using a hot iron. These were then pressed into the kames with a little fluid oil or varnish rather than cement, welded and wired to fine iron cross bars. Elsewhere in this guide, descriptions are given of some of the heraldic and other devices seen in the windows.

The Interior

The original use of some of the rooms is not known. The titles given to them are those assigned them many years ago, which continue to be used for convenience.

The Great Hall

The Great Hall and the northern part of the east range have near-identical arch-braced collar trusses and are both of c. 1504–8. They comprise the earliest parts of Little Moreton Hall. The floor would probably have been of earth strewn with rushes, there would have been a flagged, central hearth and the windows were in all probability glazed. About 1546 William Moreton II rebuilt the original service end of the Great Hall as a new wing at right angles to the main entrance passage (on the left as you enter), at the same time erecting the porch. In 1559, he inserted a new floor at gallery level (removed by 1807) and added the bay window on to the courtyard. (See p. 28 for a more detailed discussion of this complex period.)

(Below) The Great Hall

(Left) The gabled bay windows in the north-east corner of the courtyard

Screens Passage

The Great Hall is entered through the porch and the screens passage, so called because partitions running from the walls to the projecting posts or 'speres' – characteristic of the North-West – and a screen situated between these speres protected the occupants of the Great Hall from any unwelcome draughts. Screens were common and usually built as fixtures in medieval halls, but the screen here is now missing, probably because it was free-standing and moveable – like the wonderfully carved example at Rufford Old Hall, Lancashire.

Gallery

Opposite the porch door through a small door is a newel staircase to the gallery over the screens passage. Originally the gallery was open to the Great Hall and gave access to finely appointed living quarters on the first floor of the north-west wing; it was also usual (especially in the period when the screens were built) to use this area as a minstrels' gallery. The gallery wall was partitioned off *c.*1559.

Heating

The Great Hall may have been warmed by moveable braziers or an open hearth beneath a smoke canopy or louvre, which could have been situated between the main arch-braced truss in the centre of the Great Hall and a smaller truss between this and the screens passage. A vent hole in the roof recently discovered while re-roofing would have allowed smoke to escape, but as there is little evidence of soot on the timbers, it is possible the fireplace in the north wall had already been inserted.

Seating arrangements

Food was brought from the doors beyond the screens passage to the lord and his guests who sat at the 'high' end of the Hall, furthest away from the screens. The seating arrangements in medieval halls were based upon strict ideas of rank and precedence. The lord sat on the only chair (hence the name 'chairman' as a sign of rank), while the other guests were placed in diminishing order of precedence on benches at two tables against the longer side walls. This kind of seating arrangement survives in the older school and college halls, in many of which the high table is still raised on its dais. The servants' halls of some country houses also preserved a seating plan based on rank and position, reflecting the importance of the medieval hall as not only the centre of the house, but also the focus of the estate, social life and entertainment.

Floor and windows

With the end of the medieval period the importance of the Great Hall was being steadily undermined by the increasing role of private domestic accommodation within the house, and in 1559 William Moreton II modernised Little Moreton according to the new values of comfort and privacy. He inserted a floor at gallery level, to give additional accommodation at first-floor level. This floor was removed before 1807 when Cotman drew the Great Hall (illustrated on p. 43). The sawn-off remnants of the beams which supported it are visible half-way up the east or high end wall, above the doorway. The outline of a door which led from this upper room to the gallery can be discerned in the partition which runs between the two speres at first-floor level. Also in 1559 Richard Dale, carpenter, built the two great bay windows which project into the courtyard, both clearly being designed to light two floors.

Furniture

The 1563 inventory of William Moreton II's possessions lists two tables in this room, which today contains two of the three pieces of original furniture still at Little Moreton Hall: the long refectory table and the large cupboard. The 1599 inventory of John Moreton's possessions mentions 'One cubborde of boxes', and this probably refers to the large cupboard with numerous small drawers inside. Its use is unknown, but such furniture is traditionally connected with the storage of spices.

Stained glass

In bay window:

Heraldic panel bearing the arms of Brereton of Brereton. Alys Brereton from nearby Brereton married William Moreton I.

(Above) The pewter displayed in the Great Hall may include some of the pieces mentioned in the 1654 inventory

Pewter

In showcase in west wall:

The pewter, which is mostly eighteenth-century, was presented along with the furniture by Bishop Abraham in 1938. The family would have used pewter as their preferred tableware, and a set valued at £2 15s 6d was in the house in 1654.

The Parlour

In 1654 this room was called the Little Parlour. Together with the adjoining Withdrawing Room, it is structurally part of the earliest building. The roof-trusses above both rooms have mouldings almost identical to those used on the trusses of 1504–8 in the Great Hall. There were originally no ceilings to the rooms above. However, when a ceiling was added to the room above the Parlour, the floor was lowered to give additional headroom.

No hearth is mentioned in 1654, but by 1668 the Little Parlour chimney was being swept. Towards the end of her life in the 1670s, William Moreton III's widow Jane was using this room, with its fine view over the garden, as her sitting-room.

Painted decoration

This remarkable scheme was discovered in 1976 behind the Georgian panelling and conserved in 1979. It consists of simulated panelling separated from biblical scenes by an elaborate frieze, bordered above and below by a line of inter-laced ornament similar to borders found in the Chapel. The biblical scenes were painted on paper which was then pasted into position; the rest was painted directly on the plaster.

The panelling has been crudely drawn but displays elaborate paintwork, the centres of the panels being alternately red or green and grained or marbled. The vogue for such painted panelling lasted between about 1570 and 1610, at a time when wall-paintings were falling out of favour and panelling was becoming more generally accepted as an efficient and attractive insulating material: indeed, wall-paintings such

Part of the painted panelling of c.1580, discovered beneath later panelling in the Parlour

as those at Little Moreton have been and are being continually discovered behind later panelled walls. The initial 'I' for John Moreton (who died in 1598) and the Moretons' wolf's head crest can be seen in the middle section of the frieze.

It was common to place biblical scenes over the frieze, and here the subject is the story of Susanna and the Elders, from the Apocrypha. The black-letter inscriptions which summarise the story are complemented by the illustrations, the sequence being from left to right. In its barest outlines, the story runs thus: Susanna was the beautiful wife of a wealthy citizen of Babylon called Joachim. Two elderly judges who frequently visited Joachim's house on business one day saw her bathing in her husband's garden. When she refused their advances, they brought her to trial on a trumped-up charge of adultery. Susanna was about to be stoned to death when a young man called Daniel interceded on her behalf. Daniel proved that the judges' story was false, and they were condemned to death for their wickedness.

Biblical scenes such as this, which had been removed or whitewashed over in churches by Protestant reformers, were being used by Protestants in their homes as expressions of their faith and education, because English translations of the Bible made it more accessible to an increasingly literate public. Protestants discarded Catholic favourites such as the Dance of Death, the Last Judgement and the suffering and ordeals of Christ and the saints, and instead chose stories which stressed individual dilemmas and what they could do for themselves – Daniel in the Lions' Den, the Prodigal Son, the story of Susanna and the Elders, and classical themes such as the Labours of Hercules. Other Protestant creeds, namely the virtues of hard work and the power of knowledge over super-stition, are illustrated in the Long Gallery.

Doorway

The doorway (next to the fireplace) which led from the Parlour to the Great Hall was probably blocked in about 1559 when the great chimneystack was built in the Great Hall.

The Moreton wolf's head crest, from the late sixteenth-century glass in the Withdrawing Room (top) and (above) from the painted frieze in the Parlour

13

The 'great rounde table', which appears in the 1599 inventory

Furnishings

In 1654 the room was furnished with two 'leaf tables, one little table and one cupboard, ten Stooles, six cheares and four Cushions'.

The Withdrawing Room

This room, formerly known as the Old Parlour and originally part of the early sixteenth-century east range, owes much of its present appearance to improvements carried out in about 1559, when the bay window was built by Richard Dale for William Moreton II. The heavily framed and stout panelling suggests a mid-sixteenth-century date and the elaborately moulded ceiling beams are identical in section to the beams inserted in the Great Hall by William Moreton II in 1559. Jane Moreton may have used the room as a kitchen in the 1670s, when it contained spits and a dripping pan; it must then have been considered very old-fashioned.

Stained glass

Opposite the great bay which looks into the courtyard, a line of transomed windows faces east across the moat, providing a view of the farm and its cruck-framed barn, which has been dated to about 1545 by tree-ring analysis.

In right-hand light:

The wolf's head crest of the Moretons and a panel with the initials 'W.M.' (for William Moreton II) and a pun on the name Moreton: the second half – the barrel or 'tun' – still survives; the first (missing) syllable 'More' probably refers to a wolf's jaws (the Old English word 'maw', for the jaws or mouth of a voracious animal). The missing piece of glass would, therefore, have contained the bottom of the wolf's head and possibly the initials of William's wife Anne Fowleshurst.

In left-hand light:

The greyhound courant, the shield of the Moretons, surrounded by scrollwork. Some of this glass is probably late sixteenth-century.

Fireplace

The centre panel of the overmantel bears the royal arms and supporters of Queen Elizabeth. The plasterwork would originally have been coloured. Beneath the overmantel is a mid-eighteenth-century fireplace, which was built smaller than the original fireplace to facilitate the burning of coal, which was already being used here in 1654.

Furniture

The octagonal table can be identified with 'the great rounde table in the parlour' valued at 10s in the 1599 inventory. Its shape suggests it was designed to stand in one of the bay windows of 1559. In 1654 the furnishings consisted of a large table valued at £3 6s 8d (almost certainly the octagonal table), a cupboard and a little table, two chairs and a frame stool.

The Exhibition Room

At William Moreton III's death in 1654, this room was furnished as a bedroom. William's children Ann, Jane and Philip then split the house into semi-self-contained units. Ann, who occupied the Prayer Room immediately above, used it as a kitchen.

The Chapel

The Chapel was first built when the east range was extended south in about 1508: the entrance door and the mullioned window above it date to this period. The chancel was probably built in the mid-sixteenth century.

The Chapel was brought back into use in 1897 by Elizabeth Moreton following a 'Service of Reconciliation'. The same order of service was used when the kneelers (made by Cheshire WI members) were dedicated in 1977. Services continue to be held here every Sunday that the house is open during the spring and summer months.

The interior of the Chapel, sketched by James West in 1847

Stained glass

The stained glass in the chancel window, which was dedicated in July 1938, was installed by Bishop Abraham as a parting gift on handing Little Moreton over to the care of The National Trust. It was designed by Gerald Smith and reflects the previous ministry of the bishop in the Derby and Lichfield dioceses.

Painted decoration

The north and west walls of the chancel are decorated with texts which are framed by arabesques with motifs characteristic of Italian Renaissance decoration – what was called in Henry VIII's reign 'anticke work'. There are similarities in style of decoration which suggest that the work in the Parlour and the Chapel is of the same date, that is, of about 1580. When the artist James West visited Little Moreton in 1847, he drew an interlocking pattern identical to that in the midway frieze in the Parlour, which he stuck into the section of his notebook marked 'Ornaments on the beams of the Chapel'.

James West was first shown the Chapel by the groom: 'He led me across the courtyard to a door way, which I had thought was an entrance to the coal cellar, and sure enough there was a coal cellar, for what had once been the ante-chapel, was converted into a depot for coals and rubbish …' The picture shows that the chancel was tidier and West was able to draw in great detail the texts painted upon the walls. He had a professional interest in them, as he had just completed the decoration of a chapel at nearby Crewe Hall.

Timber marks

Leaving the Chapel, note the assembly marks inscribed on the timbers of the south range. These marks were made in the timbers after they had been cut, jointed and fitted together in the carpenter's yard. The timbers were then taken apart and loaded into carts, and at the building site the carpenter jointed his frame together again using the marks as a guide for assembly.

The Corn Store

Adjacent to the Chapel, but accessed from the main entry, is a dimly lit room which may have served as a lodging for a steward responsible for keeping the gate and looking after the day-to-day affairs of the estate. By the late seventeenth century, perhaps as the family fortune declined, it was converted to a more utilitarian purpose as a store. The floor was raised to protect the grain from damp and five oak-framed bins were built. These may, amongst other things, have held barley for the brew-house, latterly also wood used for fuel for the hearths. A distinctive pommel carved out of the top of each post separated the bins, although only one now survives. The room was restored and opened to visitors in 2006.

Return to the courtyard and enter the south range, which was built by William Moreton II in the 1560s. Ascend the newel staircase to the Long Gallery, passing the Guests' Hall and the Guests' Parlour on the first floor, to which you will return.

The Long Gallery

This room appears to have been conceived after construction of the south range had begun, as it is imperfectly jointed to and loaded on the first-floor ceiling joists, but there are consistencies in the form of bracing and window moulding which indicate that both were completed together. Tree-ring analysis confirms that the Long Gallery was constructed in the early 1560s, with the rest of the south range. It was included in John Moreton's inventory of 1599.

Ceiling

The massive weight of the gritstone roof was taken by the arch-braced roof trusses, in which curved braces are morticed and tenoned into the straight principal rafters and the collar (serving to pull the whole together). This gave more headroom than the conventional 'closed truss' and was also aesthetically pleasing, like the semi-circular wind-braces, which are finely cusped in a local fashion also seen at Smithills and Rufford Old Hall, both early Tudor Lancashire houses.

The crossbeams running between the roof-trusses were probably inserted in the seventeenth century in an attempt to prevent the structure from bursting apart. They may also have been meant to support a ceiling, which was up before 1658, when it was discovered that 'there lyes in the false roof over the gallery one great saddle one pair of sterrops one girth and one bridleraynes and one large bit'. It was subsequently taken down. In the 1890s Elizabeth Moreton inserted iron tie-rods as an additional precautionary measure.

Plaster work

At either end of the Long Gallery are plaster-work renderings of Destiny and Fortune, taken from the 1556 edition of *The Castle of Knowledge*. This was a treatise on the sphere written by the

The figures of Destiny (below) and Fortune (overleaf) in the Long Gallery plasterwork were taken from the title-page of Robert Recorde's 'The Castle of Knowledge' (1556) (right)

The Long Gallery

(Above) Fortune, from the Long Gallery plasterwork

mathematician Robert Recorde (*c*.1510–58), who invented the = sign. At the east end of the Long Gallery, the figure of Destiny holds aloft the sphere in one hand, and in the other hand she clasps a pair of open dividers. At the west end, Fortune is blindfolded, and therefore impartial, and stands on a globe which suggests her power over the world as well as her natural instability. In accordance with the iconography intended by Recorde, Fortune would have originally held a string attached to the hub of the Wheel of Fortune. But although these allegorical figures are identical to those portrayed on the frontispiece of Recorde's book, the accompanying texts differ so much that one is tempted to say that the plasterer obtained his information from some secondhand source – such as a pattern book. Thus in place of Recorde's motto 'The Sphere of destinye whose governour is Knowledge', the text at the east end of the Long Gallery reads, 'The Speare of Destinye whose Ruler is Knowledge'. At the other end of the Gallery, the text is 'The Wheele of Fortune whose Rule [in place of 'ruler'] is Ignorance'. Despite these errors of interpretation, the belief by Protestants that individual striving and knowledge, rather than the blind acceptance of Fate, would determine one's destiny, is here plain for all to see. Knowledge of science and the New World were much admired in the Elizabethan age.

Furniture

When first built, the Long Gallery would have been sparsely furnished, for the Elizabethans used such rooms for daily exercise and games – four early seventeenth-century tennis balls have been recovered from behind the panelling here. The inventory of 1654 reveals that it was once furnished with 'one safe [a hanging cupboard for food], two great blew cheeres with sides', 'five lesser cheeres blew' and no fewer than sixteen 'blew stooles'.

The Upper Porch Room

This room was called the Gallery Chamber in the 1654 inventory and was probably intended to be a sanctuary from the fun and games of the Long Gallery.

Fireplace

The central panel contains the Moreton arms, quartered by the cross of the Macclesfield family. This was in celebration of the prudent marriage in 1329 of John de Moreton to Margaret, co-heiress to the estate of John de Macclesfield. This panel is flanked by the figures of Justice with scales, and Mercy with an open book.

Furniture

In 1654 it was furnished as a bedroom, like the Lower Porch Room directly below. The furnishings included a curtained and carved bed, a chest, and a chair, stool and cupboard, all upholstered en suite in green cloth.

Descend the stairs to the first landing and turn left.

The Guests' Parlour

By 1654 this was called 'Mr Booth's Chamber' and seems to have been used regularly by Jack Booth of Tremlowe, who was not only a cousin but also a close friend of William Moreton III.

Fireplace

The overmantel is elaborately panelled.

Furniture

The 1654 inventory mentions a grate and two bedsteads, one with basic bedding, but Mr Booth probably had some of his possessions in the room, which would not have been listed.

Near the entrance to the room a discreet doorway in the panelling gives access to the Brew-house Chamber.

The Brew-house Chamber

This room formed the top floor of the block which was built on to the north-west end of the south range in the early seventeenth century as a brew-house and bake-house. When first constructed, the room was probably servants' accommodation and may have been accessed through a hatch in the ceiling of the brew-house below.

A passage leads to a garderobe tower with two closets, all with their original seats on both ground and first floors.

These garderobes and the others positioned about Little Moreton Hall were little more than elaborate earth closets, the effluent being collected and used as fertilizer or, in the case of the south-range garderobe, being flushed directly through holes at the base of the cess chamber into the moat.

On the other side of the landing is the Guests' Hall.

The Guests' Hall and Porch Room

When first conceived, access between the Guests' Hall and the Guests' Parlour would have been on the same level. The massive carved consoles, one tree-ring-dated to c.1660, were inserted both as decoration and to help support the load of the Long Gallery above.

In the seventeenth century this room was called the Joiner's Chamber, probably because of the quality of the panelling. It and the adjoining Porch Room were probably used by Edward Moreton's brother Philip when he was at home in the 1640s; several years later he kept his books in the closet here. The panelled partition was inserted in the eighteenth century.

Floor

The lime-ash flooring, used on the first floor at Little Moreton Hall, and the plaster infill between the timbers, would have made an effective barrier against fire, which always threatened timber framed buildings.

Lime and ash were worked together until moist and then rammed down on to a bedding of straw and laths. The section of floor on the left as you enter the room was replaced in 2002 following careful analysis of the constituent materials. The original oak laths were retained and some of the old lime-ash was able to be ground down and re-used in the new floor.

Furniture

According to the 1654 inventory, the Guests' Hall was sparsely furnished, but the Porch Room had a bed and a little table.

(Right) One of the garderobe closets

(Above)   The Prayer Room

Through the doorway in the north-east corner is the Prayer Room.

The Prayer Room

This occupied the south end of the extension added to the east range *c.*1508, which also contains the Chapel. In the early seventeenth century it was the chamber of William Moreton III's daughter Ann. The next room housed her maid.

The room takes its present name from the belief that it was used by the Moreton family to participate in services taking place in the Chapel below. Part of the east wall seems to have been removed and replaced by vertical timbers and a wide window (now plastered over), which would have provided a view down into the chancel. This can only have been short-lived, as painted text in the chancel, which is of the late-sixteenth century, covers the other side of the wall.

Ceiling

The ceiling was inserted in the late sixteenth century, having previously been open to fine arch-braced roof-trusses which are now obscured from view. When the ceiling was inserted, one of these arch braces was removed: the mortice hole can still be seen in the west wall.

Furniture

Ann Moreton furnished the room with a great bedstead with 'five blew curtaynes and a vallence'. Under it was a trundle bed. There was another bed with two red curtains and a 'canabye', and a little table. A great press stood against the wall with a cupboard at the end of it. The west-facing window was curtained, probably to keep the sun out, and a large chest stood under it.

The doorway at the north end opens on to a newel staircase which leads back to the courtyard.

The Garden and Estate

History

Although it is likely that a garden always formed part of the surroundings of the hall, no documentary evidence is available before the early seventeenth century, when a set of accounts refers to a gardener, to the buying of seeds and to putting in an apple tree. However, Philip Moreton, who ran the estate for his brother in the mid-seventeenth century, took a considerable interest in the garden and from his notebooks much information on the layout of the area within the moat can be gleaned.

The present garden lies on the site of its seventeenth-century predecessor. This earlier garden was surrounded by what Philip called a wall, but was almost certainly a paling fence, covered on both sides with hooks for espaliered fruit trees. These included a number of plum trees and a bergamot pear. There was a border under the wall where Philip planted 29 'collyflowers', and a door, which led out to the moat side, where the wall adjoined the Little Parlour. The rest of the garden, in typical seventeenth-century fashion, was divided into quarters, and the quarters into beds.

At least one of these beds held herbs – sweet marjoram and 'cardus' seeds were mentioned; in another notebook Philip records, 'I set 10 large beans'. But flowers had a place too, and Thomas Stevenson, who worked intermittently in the garden, was paid for 'removing some Julyflower setts'.

Within the garden area there was a nursery in which young trees were nurtured until the time came for them to be transferred to the orchard. Another nursery, 'att side of the ould Dogkennell', was set with '30 slipps of the dwarf apple'. The orchard itself seems to have been on the west of the house, where the orchard is today. Against the Brew-house wall, sheltered from the east wind, a border was dug in 1668 and an 'Apricock tree' planted. It may well be that the orchard had suffered from neglect, for in autumn 1663 the orchard wall had to be rebuilt by Randle Tomson the carpenter.

The mount, such a feature of the present orchard, is not recorded in the documents. It is thought to have been created in the sixteenth

Artist's impression of the working landscape at Little Moreton c.1550. At this date the south range of the house had not been built

Little Moreton Hall

century, to provide a vantage point from which to view a knot garden, patterned and divided into beds much as Philip Moreton's garden was divided. There are two such mounts at Little Moreton, the second outside the moat to the south-west. Both are of similar size to the mount in the enclosed garden at Boscobel in Shropshire, on which stood a small wooden summer-house. A larger mount, in the same position by the moat as the mount inside the garden at Little Moreton, is shown in Kip and Knyff's 1697 view of Dunham Massey, near Altrincham, about 20 miles away. The mount at Dunham, which still exists, was encircled by three bands of hedging and surmounted, as at Boscobel, by a gabled summer-house.

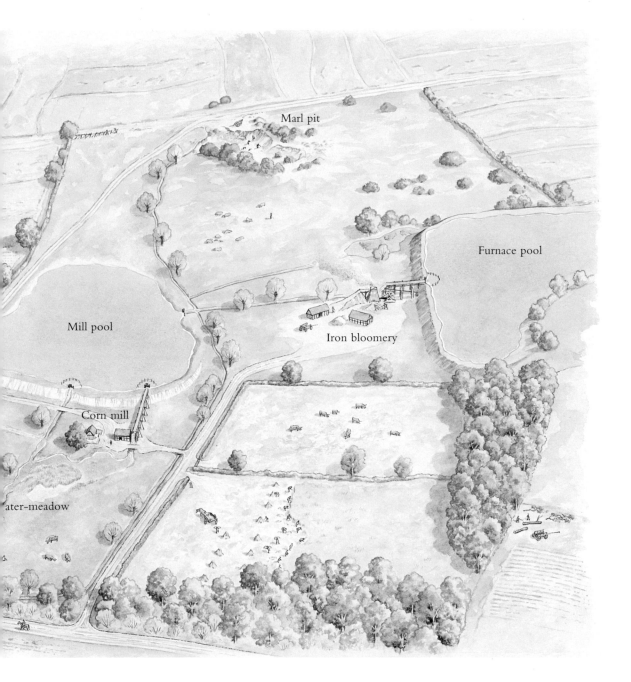

Marl pit

Furnace pool

Mill pool

Iron bloomery

Corn mill

ater-meadow

(Above) The Knot Garden

(Right) The Knot Garden was based on this design from Loenard Meagre's 'The English Gardener' (1670)

The second and larger mount, at the south-west angle of the moat, in the seventeenth century gave its name to the Mount Yard, an enclosed grassy area between the present car-park and the path up to the moat bridge. Next to it, where the car-park is today, lay the 'ould cowfield', where, before cowhouses became accepted agricultural practice in the middle of the seventeenth century, the cows were held for milking.

The main farmyard (now in private hands) lies to the east of the house. There is a fine sixteenth-century barn and a cowhouse, put up in the 1650s and renovated in the 1790s, when the carthouse next door was added to the range. In addition the seventeenth-century farmstead boasted a stable for the farm horses, an 'oxehouse' for the team of oxen, a 'wainhouse' behind the farmyard, and a dovecot.

The fortunes of the estate were not dependent solely on the farm. From the late fifteenth century the Moretons had owned a bloomsmithy, a medieval iron-working site where iron was forged under water-powered hammers. The mill lay across the fields to the south-east of the house and was powered from a great pool, the dam of which can still be seen. Another mill, this time for corn, was sited on the far side of the field in front of the house. The pool for this concern lay opposite the farmyard and the contours are still visible. The bloomsmithy, which was always let to tenants, disappeared during the early eighteenth century. The cornmill survived until the early nineteenth century, when the Moretons refused to restore the decaying fabric.

The seventeenth-century Moretons had a share in a coal pit, for which they employed contract labour with complicated stipulations about the good coal and the 'sleck' (dross). They also quarried for and dressed mill-stones; again the work was subcontracted, with a clause limiting the workers to '2 pickmen'.

As the century went on, timber production and fish-farming seem to have become increasingly important, and, with the farm and the rents from cottage property, were the main sources of income in the eighteenth century. In addition to the specialised stew-ponds, the moat and mill-ponds were used for breeding carp and tench. For this reason the 'Smithy Pool' survived long after the bloomsmithy had vanished.

Tour of the Garden

From the courtyard, there is a view west to the orchard, round which has been established a mixed hedge of Hornbeam, Holly, Quickthorn, Honeysuckle and Sweet Briar. Traditional fruits such as apples, pears, quinces and medlars all grow well here.

The Knot and nearby Yew Tunnel were laid out in 1972, with the support of a grant from the Leverhulme Trust. No knot gardens have survived intact from the sixteenth and seventeenth centuries, partly because they demand a great deal of labour, and partly because by Charles II's reign the parterre had become more fashionable. However, knot designs do survive and that at Little Moreton is based on a design in *The English Gardener*, published by Leonard Meager in 1670, though probably Elizabethan in origin. It takes the form of an 'open knot', that is to say gravel is used in the spaces between the Dwarf Box hedges. In the borders at each end of the knot, set out in a regular pattern, are many period flowering plants, some of which are good forms of native species. Planted under the standard gooseberries are *Galium odoratum* (Woodruff); *Teucrium chamaedrys* (Germander); *Origanum vulgare* 'Aureum' (Golden Marjoram); *Armeria maritima* (Thrift); *Iberis sempervirens* (Candytuft); *Ajuga reptans* 'Atropurpurea' (Bugle); *Fragaria vesca* (Wild Strawberry); *Chamaemelum nobile* 'Flore Pleno' (Chamomile); *Saxifraga umbrosa* (London Pride); *Hyssopus officinalis* (Hyssop); and *Lamium maculatum*. The standard gooseberries are replacements for standard Old English Lavenders which sadly succumbed to the cold damp winters. Also included in the borders are a number of favourite 'cottage garden' plants, eg *Tradescantia virginiana* (Spiderwort); *Paeonia officinalis* (Peony); *Iris germanica* (London Flag); *Geum rivale* (Water Avens); *Lychnis viscaria* 'Plena' (Catchfly) and *Geranium sanguineum* (Bloody Crane's-bill).

The opportunity has been taken in the house borders to plant a few period plants, such as *Lunaria rediviva* (Honesty); *Dryopteris filix-mas* (Male Fern); *Tiarella cordifolia* (Foam Flower) and *Astrantia major* (Masterwort), but the emphasis here is on bold planting of labour-saving plants.

On the north and east sides of the Knot Garden are four beds which are now planted with vegetables and herbs of the Elizabethan period.

The Building of Little Moreton

The name Moreton is believed to be of Anglo-Saxon origin from the old English or old Norse 'mor' meaning marshland and 'tune' meaning a farmstead. These two elements go together to form the word 'Mortune' meaning 'a farm at a marsh'. The area is called Little Moreton to distinguish it from its greater neighbour Moreton-cum-Alcumlow or Greater Moreton, which was a township rather than a simple farmstead. It would appear from the Domesday Book entry that the area had suffered much from the period of unrest following the Norman Conquest in 1066. Land that had been worth twenty shillings in Edward the Confessor's time was now valued at only two, and it seems to have been largely waste with a relatively small amount of woodland. Two enclosures and a hawk's eyrie are also mentioned.

The Moretons of Little Moreton Hall were descended from the marriage in 1216 of Lettice de Moreton with Sir Gralam de Lostock. Little Moreton was part of the patrimony of the de Lostocks as sub-tenants of the Barons of Halton. Sir Gralam's eldest son Richard, presumably because his own sons died young, settled the Moreton part of his inheritance on his younger brother Geoffrey de Lostock, by a mid-thirteenth-century deed which was still in the possession of the Moreton family in 1815. It is thus Geoffrey who first became 'de Moreton', a name continued by his son Gralam, who inherited around 1280.

These early Moretons emerge from the surviving sources as a difficult and argumentative clan, perhaps because the most readily available records are legal documents. In the mid-fifteenth century, for example, Sir Richard de Moreton was bound over to keep the King's peace, several neighbours standing surety for him. No evidence survives of the house occupied by Sir Richard or his ancestors, but it may well have been on the same site as the present building.

Richard's grandson William Moreton I seems to have inherited some of his grandfather's belligerence. In 1513 he was involved in a quarrel with Thomas Rode of nearby Odd Rode 'concerning which of theym should sit highest in churche and foremost goe in procession'. This affair had to be settled by an arbitrator, William Brereton of Brereton, who allowed the precedence to him who 'may dispende in landes by title of inheritance 10 marke or above more than the other'; this turned out to be William Moreton. Not surprisingly, Rode refused to accept the verdict, complaining that Moreton and Brereton were related. The case was probably heard in the magnificent church of Astbury, about three miles north-west of Little Moreton Hall, where a considerable amount of stained glass was installed by the Moreton family in the fifteenth century.

It was William Moreton I who was responsible for the earliest surviving parts of Little Moreton, the east range and the Great Hall, which have been shown by tree-ring dating to have been constructed in the first decade of the sixteenth century. The east wing at the 'high end' of the Great Hall was probably always used for domestic accommodation, although blocked doors between the Parlour and the Hall and between the Great Hall and the courtyard indicate slight changes in the layout, probably occurring at the time of the 1559 remodelling.

By this time the Moretons' estates were almost twice as extensive as they had been 150 years earlier, covering 1,360 acres and including three water-mills. Prosperity enabled the Moretons, especially William Moreton II (d. 1563) and his son John (d. 1598), to extend and modernise the house. About 1546, William II built the north-west wing, porch and gallery. The north-west wing probably succeeded an earlier service range on the site, while the porch and gallery were added into the existing screens passage – that is the space between the spere truss and the new wing. The first floor of the north-west wing contains three interconnected chambers: one had access to two garderobes and another (the north chamber) still has its fine brick fireplace and impressive arch-braced roof with cusped wind-braces. The first floor of the east range also contains two chambers with arch-braced roof-trusses, which were open to view before they were blocked by the insertion of ceilings in the late sixteenth century.

A decade and a half later, further and more fashionable work was carried out for William Moreton II by Richard Dale. The inscriptions on Richard Dale's beautiful bay windows firmly date this work to 1559 as follows:

God is Al in Al Thing: This windous Whire made by William Moreton in the yeare of oure Lorde m.d.lix.

Below this was added the line:

Rycharde Dale Carpeder made thies windous by the grac of God.

These bay windows displayed glass, a rare luxury then, to the best possible effect, and the opportunity was taken further to enhance domestic comfort by inserting a first floor and refurbishing the Withdrawing Room. If not

The plaster coat of arms on the Upper Porch Room chimney-piece celebrates the marriage in 1329 of John de Moreton and the heiress Margaret de Macclesfield

(Above) The Gatehouse and south range

already built, a fireplace was inserted in the Hall and a window replaced in the Prayer Room.

We know that Richard Dale's son Richard worked at Congleton church and built a fine new porch at Nantwich grammar school in 1612: he was a travelling craftsman, although his inventory of 1637 shows that he also farmed to supplement his income. Carpenters of their calibre would have been able to act as business-men and administrators as well as choosing trees for timber and making scale drawings. The elder Richard Dale evidently discussed work in hand with his patron, for in his will of 1563 William Moreton II requested that the work at Little Moreton was to be completed 'according to the devyse thereof devysed twixt me and Richard Dale the head wright and workman off the same frame'.

William Moreton must have been referring to the building of the south range, and the beams there are identical to Richard Dale's work in the Great Hall and the Withdrawing Room. The Long Gallery may not have been part of the original design but there is no sign of roof-trusses having been removed from above first-floor level. The most likely and generally accepted explanation is that the Long Gallery was added as an afterthought: perched on the first floor, the Gallery not only commands excellent views of the surrounding countryside, but also enhances the visual appeal of Little Moreton.

An increase of domestic comfort and infor-mality characterised the period of William's son, John Moreton, up to his death in 1598. He must have been responsible for decorating the Parlour and the Chapel chancel in about 1580. The chancel itself must have been built before this date, very probably at the same time or after the ceiling was inserted in the Prayer Room. The last major extension occurred in the early seventeenth century with the building of the Kitchen and Brew-house range in the south-west corner of the courtyard.

The doorway of the porch leading into the Great Hall

The Moreton Family

With the accession of John Moreton's eldest son William III (1574–1654) in 1598, the history of the Moreton family becomes less obscure. William was married the same year, when he was 23, to Jane, daughter of Thomas Lancaster and widow of a friend of the family, Richard Massey. Jane was a considerable heiress and exhaustive negotiations were put in hand to ensure that she was really entitled to her inheritance. William and Jane were certainly to need the money, for during their married lives they seem to have acted as bankers to a large extended family.

Hardly had William's own marriage taken place than arrangements had to be put in hand for the marriage of young Dorothy Massey, child of Jane's first marriage. William and Jane chose Thomas Leversage, the young son of a neighbour, as the bridegroom, and a betrothal contract was drawn up, hedged about with financial stipulations in case the children repudiated the agreement, as they were entitled to do when they reached the age of fourteen; Thomas was then not yet ten. In the meantime, land was exchanged and a new house built at Cockshute, just down the road from Little Moreton Hall, so that Dorothy could live near her mother.

This warm sense of family permeates the Moreton documents. Cousinship was taken seriously and William's sea-faring cousin Matthew made it clear that he relied far more heavily on William's goodwill than on that of his own brothers. William's unmarried sister, Mary, spent her life at Moreton, receiving an allowance from her brother, and his brother Tobias, Uncle Toby to the family, lived in the house in his old age.

William's own family was large; he and Jane had nine surviving children, five sons and four daughters. The eldest, John, was the black sheep of the family and must have been a severe disappointment to his parents. He was sent up to Christ's College, Cambridge in 1614, when he was seventeen, but two years later his college tutor wrote to recommend his removal: 'I now despair of his well-doing here … your young gentleman was got to a bad house by Peterhouse together with another rakestrel.' John, who had been drinking, refused to come back to his lodgings and declared that 'he cared not if he never see Moreton more'. He felt just the same when sober; it is clear from his subsequent behaviour that he wanted no responsibility for family or estate. He favoured a London life and although not estranged from the family, made rare visits to the family home.

William, the second boy, was originally destined for the law and placed with a 'master', but he too was not interested in the learned life and, aided and abetted by his 'Uncle' Matthew, wrote to his father:

I founde myselfe more inclined to an other kinde of life. Whereof lovinge father I entreate you to fulfil and graunt me my desire that is to give me leave to follow the sea … I think my maister will be contente to take another of my brothers in steede of mee if you will but give your consent there unto for this course of life I cannot undergo.

Perhaps mindful of the trouble caused by John, he signed himself, 'Your obedient son till death'.

Since William was going to sea, John was fired with a desire to do likewise; there was talk of his joining an expedition to the Amazon, but only as a gentleman adventurer not as a mere seaman. His father appears to have refused the necessary £50 stake. When, after a number of setbacks, William sailed for the West Indies with his uncle, as purser's mate in the *Unity*, John was left behind. He continued an expensive life in London, despite the misgivings of his family, and in 1621 made a disastrous marriage. The letter he wrote to his parents, entreating their forgiveness for his 'rash and unfortunate marriage' and likening himself to the prodigal son, is only the first of a number of similar letters written when John was short of money. He was described as 'of a low stature, verie slender and leane faced'.

It was John's marriage that finally made

(Above) 'The cupborde of boxes' (probably a spice cupboard), which is listed in the 1599 inventory

William Moreton III realise that he was in no way suited to head the family and to put in train the machinery to disinherit him. It is typical of the man that he did this reluctantly. John himself wrote, 'Your unwillingness to deprive mee of my inheritance … I can impute to nothing but your tender conscience.' The problem was complicated by the younger William's absences abroad and the estate was finally settled, not on William, but on his younger brother Edward in 1627.

Edward Moreton was a complex character. Academically able, he was the only one of the Moreton sons to go to Eton. From there he went first to Cambridge in 1619 and then to Oxford, where he obtained his MA in 1626. Money was tight; his letters home are full of his need to buy books. In addition he was trying every means at his disposal to get a living to augment his fellowship, badgering acquaintances in high places to help him, but without success.

During this difficult period Edward lent heavily on Peter, his junior by a year. Peter had joined him at Cambridge only a couple of months after he himself had gone up there. Peter seems in all ways to have been an admirable young man, approved by his tutor, considerate of his parents and concerned for his brothers. After some initial difficulties – it seems that finding suitable employment was no easier in the seventeenth century – he eventually secured a post as private secretary to Sir Isaac Wake, the British Ambassador in Venice. On his arrival in Italy Wake sent him 'to Florence (where the best language is spoken)', and found him 'apt to learne'. The most tantalising event of Peter's career occurred in 1627 when, unable to return to Italy from England due to war on the Continent, he heard that there was 'a gentleman going speedilie into Italy from the King about Pictures and som such employment'. This was none other than Nicholas Lanier, Master of the King's Music and a prominent connoisseur, who was on his way to arrange the purchase of the Duke of Mantua's collection for Charles I.

(Left)
A seventeenth-century console bracket in the Guests' Hall

(Opposite)
The west end of the south range

Moreton managed to take advantage of Lanier's special pass, and travelled with him as far as Venice. His father, William Moreton III, seems also to have been involved with Lanier's mission, acting as an intermediary between him and the ambassador.

On Sir Isaac Wake's death in 1632, Peter was forced to spend some months in London seeking employment. He used that time to further not only his own career, but those of Edward and his youngest brother Philip, who was then twenty and seeking a place in chambers. William was also in London, looking for an opportunity to go abroad. All the brothers seem to have fore-gathered at the house of Richard Parnall, a tailor, where John, William and Philip had all lodged at one time or another and where Parnall seems to have kept a kindly eye on them.

These were difficult years for the younger members of the family and expensive years for their parents. Even Peter was unable to manage without his quarterly allowance of £5 from his father and had eventually to take a temporary post as tutor to Lord Desmond, with whom he set out to tour Italy in 1633.

Edward became depressed at his lack of prospects and retired to Moreton. Lord Goring, who had been trying to help him, wrote, speaking of his sickness of body and mind and urging him not to bury his talents in the ground. Philip was still unemployed. John continued to worry his parents by his way of life and in 1633 William wrote from a tobacco plantation in Virginia complaining that the clothes he had been promised 'last year in the Scipio' had never arrived so that he was reduced to rags. To add to these worries his half-sister Dorothy, 'sister Leversage', embarrassed the family by being taken to court to answer charges of dishonest dealing in some property dispute. Peter wrote, 'I shall blush and account myself scandalised in having hir soe foule faults published in such a place'.

Then, in 1634, the situation began to improve. John was provided with some sort of post, although he complained bitterly to his parents that no one had written to him since he had 'come to a strange place to reside at your pleasure'. Edward received the Yorkshire living of Grinton, and at the beginning of the following year Philip got his longed-for place in chambers, although 'my m[aste]r att the beginning had not ymplyment for two clarkes'.

Peter became English Agent in Turin at a salary of £160 a year. In the summer of 1635, 'Cousin' John Eardisley visited him there and reported to William senior that Peter 'lives in as brave respecte as can be, more liker a prince than a subject and doeth assure me that you may take as great coumfort in him as a father can doe from a son'. Such news must have cheered and reassured William and Jane. Unfortunately the document sealed with the Privy Seal which entitled Peter to his salary was mislaid and once again William Moreton had to turn provider.

More good news was to come. In 1636 Edward married Margaret Webb, the daughter of Sir William Webb, a friend of Peter and the niece of Archbishop Laud. It would appear that the union was a happy one. In December of that year a cousin wrote archly to William, 'I may not forget my service to Dr Morton and his best beloved'. The following year saw the fruits of Edward's many endeavours to find a better living. Lord Coventry made good his promise of help, appointing Edward his chaplain; he became rector of Tattenhall in Cheshire and a prebendary of Chester Cathedral and, in 1639, vicar of Sefton in Lancashire, where he and Margaret made their home.

William Moreton's daughters may well have suffered from the continual drain on the family resources in the 1620s and '30s. Only Elizabeth was married young – in 1621, when she was nineteen – to Randle Rode, who lived a mile or so from Moreton. Mary, the youngest girl, seems to have been choosy, and various approaches were made which came to nothing. She was finally married when she was 27 to Jonathan Woodnoth, a friend of the family who must have been considerably older than she was. The other two daughters, Ann and Jane, remained unmarried. A relative wrote of Ann, 'She is of a sober and differit carriage and attendes upon her booke dilligently and in few wordes.' Despite this propriety she had a great love of finery, and tailor's bills and lists of Ann's wardrobe, including red and green 'taffety' petticoats and red jersey stockings, exist among the family papers. We know little of Jane, except that she had a sharp tongue.

William's wife Jane died in 1637. In 1642, when the Civil War broke out, William was living at Moreton with his sister Mary, his brother Tobias, his two daughters and his cousin 'Jack' Booth, of Tremlowe, the Cheshire genealogist who was so much part of the household that he had his own room in the south range.

It is from Cousin Booth that we first hear of William Moreton's imprisonment and release in the early days of the Civil War. He wrote from Tremlowe of his anxiety to see his friend, but was too sick to ride all the way to Moreton. In London Philip had been equally concerned:

'I understand from my sister Ann her letter that you have obtained your liberty and that you are in good health and have been since your imprisonment.' Just why William was imprisoned we do not know, but it is reasonable to assume that it was due directly or indirectly to his support of the Royalist cause.

The family continued to suffer for its Royalist sympathies. Edward's main living at Sefton was sequestered in 1643. The same year the Moreton estate was confiscated and William and Edward were apparently required to live at enemy headquarters, leaving Ann and Jane to wrestle with the problems of the estate. It seems that the Parliamentary Committee was prepared to lease the estate back to the daughters but continued to harass them, refusing to continue paying

The east side of the inner courtyard

annuities and demanding settlement before the due date. Cattle and goods were distrained and exorbitant rates demanded for their redemption. In the absence of William and Edward, the women, 'who have only a fifth part not amounting to xxli a yeare for the livelyhood and support of their aged father & themselves', had to rely on their neighbour and relative, John Bellott, to advise them and write out, 'as well as I can make it', a suitable petition for restitution. It seems that the application was eventually successful, for the rent was reduced and the annuities due to Aunt Mary and brother John were taken into consideration.

By 1644 William had returned home in time to deal with another drain on the family's weakened resources. He worked out that in August and September of that year 316 meals had been consumed by Parliamentary soldiers billeted on the house, with hay for 225 horses. He sent the bill, written in his fine italic hand, to the Parliamentary Committee in Nantwich.

By 1645 the family finances were in a parlous state. The heavy expenses of the pre-war period meant that the estate was already in trouble at the beginning of the war. Now the farms were neglected, heavy fines had taken a further toll and the cost of settling the estate came to £641. Attempts to break the entail and sell the whole property failed, but Cuttleford farm and other land was sold and the Lower Mill mortgaged. The remainder of the property, the hall and its contents and the demesne, was transferred to Ann, Jane and Philip; Edward was to pay for all reasonable repairs. Despite these efforts, when William III died in September 1654, he left debts of between £3,000 and £4,000, and to cover at least some of these liabilities the remainder of the estate had to be mortgaged to John Bellott for £1,000. The inventory made of Little Moreton after William's death describes a house well, if not sumptuously, furnished. The Long Gallery, which today, like most of the rooms, is bare of furniture, contained a large set of seat furniture, upholstered in blue. The main bedrooms were liberally supplied with feather-beds, pillows, blankets, bed-hangings and curtains, most often in shades of red and green.

During these troubled years, it seems that Edward was at Moreton very little, despite losing his livings, spending his time at Sefton Hall where perhaps he acted as private chaplain. Much of the burden fell on Philip Moreton, now well established in his legal practice. Although his professional expertise was greatly in demand throughout the family – Mary's husband also suffered the sequestration of his estate – Phillip gradually gave up his London-based practice to become his brother's agent at Moreton. It is from his memoranda books, tiny notebooks written between 1646 and 1669, that most of our information on the day-to-day workings of the estate can be gleaned. They also contain details of the books Philip bought, what he paid when he stayed with his 'sister Leversage' or dined with his brother Peter on his periodic visits to London; how he changed Aunt Mary's silver thimble ('md that I put the thymble into the money bagg') or bought his sister Jane a pair of Spanish leather shoes. They record the payment for the ringers at William's funeral, the deaths of Peter and John in 1658 and 1662, and of 'my deare sister Ann' in 1658.

By 1660, when the monarchy was restored, only Philip and Jane were living permanently at Moreton, but they were regularly joined by Edward's children, who appear to have relied upon Uncle Philip and Aunt Jane for a succession of favours. Jane's serious illness in 1668 called forth a flurry of letters between Sefton, Moreton and Oxford, where William, Edward's eldest, was studying, and great rejoicing when her health improved. William appears to have been particularly close to his uncle, confiding that he has written 'a simple little piece' – perhaps a love poem – which he does not want shown to all and sundry and begging Philip to forward a watch, given to him by a 'lady', which he dare not admit he has left behind.

Edward himself was becoming more frail and more irascible, quarrelling with the Dean of Chester and requiring skilful management by his wife and family. Margaret Moreton wrote to Philip, 'I shall doe my best to prevent him going earlier to Chester or to doe anything els that should doe him any harm but you know his temper when he is set one.' A postscript, 'My

William Moreton, Bishop of Kildare and Meath (1641–1715); by Michael Dahl (Christ Church, Oxford)

Husb: hath altered his mind', shows the success of her diplomacy. In fact, Edward was to outlast Philip by some years. In 1668, Philip too was in poor health; Doll Rode, his sister Elizabeth's daughter, several times sent him 'egg water' as a remedy for gallstones and he died the following year in October 1669. Jane continued to live at the house until her death in 1674.

Edward died in February 1674, leaving Moreton to Margaret and then to William, but by this date William was well set on a clerical career which would lead him to an Irish bishopric. Moreton was therefore let to Randle Rode, Elizabeth Moreton's husband, the Rodes having sold nearby Rode Hall to Roger Wilbraham in 1669.

In 1677 William Moreton accompanied James, Duke of Ormonde, Lord Lieutenant of Ireland, to Dublin as his chaplain. Almost immediately he was appointed Dean of Christchurch, Dublin, and in 1682 he was made Bishop of Kildare, although six years later, at the overthrow of James II, it is recorded that he 'fled to England and there continued until that nation was settled'. He was subsequently translated to Meath and made a Commissioner of the Great Seal by Queen Anne. During this time he married twice; by his first wife, Mary, he had a son, Richard, and a daughter, Annabella. His second wife, also a Mary, gave him two more children, William and Mary. Bishop Moreton died in Dublin in 1716.

Although Richard was the elder son, he passed his title to the Moreton estate to his half-brother, William V, who having attended Trinity College, Dublin, was then in the Inner Temple, London. It would appear that William was no stranger to Moreton. The main part of the house and the farmland was let to tenants, but a clause provided for the owner to take up residence again if six months' notice was given, and certain rooms were expressly excluded from the lease, namely the 'little parlour, the Roome over it, the Gallery and Gallery chamber and the study'. There is no indication that William Moreton ever lived permanently at Little Moreton, but he certainly retained the use of these rooms, which were described much later in his will as 'the Several Appartments hereto-fore kept for my use'. They were provided with plate, utensils and furniture, and it seems clear that they were used often enough to justify their exclusion from any agreement. They were probably occupied by William's mother, Mary, later Lady Jones, described as of 'London, late of further Moreton', in the Astbury burial registers. Other friends of the family were allowed to use the apartments in the owner's absence. No attempt was made to modernise what was already by the eighteenth century a venerable building, but minor modifications to the fabric continued. The sash windows in the Parlour and the fireplaces there and in the Withdrawing Room were inserted in the middle of the century.

Later letters show that William Moreton was well acquainted with his Cheshire property. He had local friends and his second wife, Jane, was from Lawton, less than two miles from Little Moreton Hall. He was also anxious to add to his estate and, in 1752, bought land at Smallwood, including Arclid Hall for £3,500. Nevertheless, William Moreton spent most of his time in London, where he held a succession of legal offices in the City, before being unanimously elected and admitted Recorder of London in 1753. Two years later he became a Member of Parliament and he was knighted the same year.

Lady Moreton died in 1758 and Sir William in 1763. He was then in his 67th year and had no surviving children. He left his property to his nephew, Richard Taylor, son of his half-sister Annabella on condition that he changed his name to Moreton. So the name of house and owner remained the same, although for the first time in seventeen generations the link of direct succession through the male line had been broken.

Family Tree

Owners of Little Moreton
are in CAPITALS

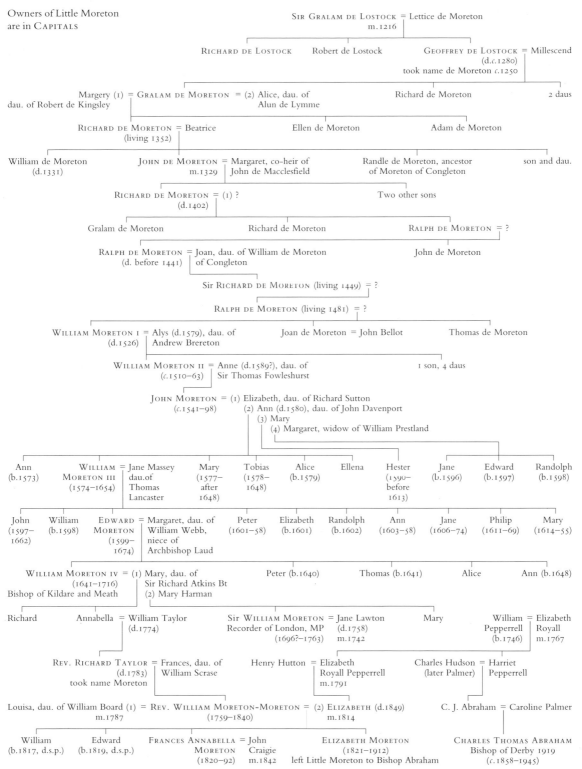

SIR GRALAM DE LOSTOCK = Lettice de Moreton
m.1216

RICHARD DE LOSTOCK   Robert de Lostock   GEOFFREY DE LOSTOCK = Millescend
(d.c.1280)
took name de Moreton c.1250

Margery (1) = GRALAM DE MORETON = (2) Alice, dau. of   Richard de Moreton   2 daus
dau. of Robert de Kingsley   Alun de Lymme

RICHARD DE MORETON = Beatrice   Ellen de Moreton   Adam de Moreton
(living 1352)

William de Moreton   JOHN DE MORETON = Margaret, co-heir of   Randle de Moreton, ancestor   son and dau.
(d.1331)   m.1329 | John de Macclesfield   of Moreton of Congleton

RICHARD DE MORETON = (1) ?   Two other sons
(d.1402)

Gralam de Moreton   Richard de Moreton   RALPH DE MORETON = ?

RALPH DE MORETON = Joan, dau. of William de Moreton   John de Moreton
(d. before 1441) | of Congleton

Sir RICHARD DE MORETON (living 1449) = ?

RALPH DE MORETON (living 1481) = ?

WILLIAM MORETON I = Alys (d.1579), dau. of   Joan de Moreton = John Bellot   Thomas de Moreton
(d.1526) | Andrew Brereton

WILLIAM MORETON II = Anne (d.1589?), dau. of   1 son, 4 daus
(c.1510–63) | Sir Thomas Fowleshurst

JOHN MORETON = (1) Elizabeth, dau. of Richard Sutton
(c.1541–98)   (2) Ann (d.1580), dau. of John Davenport
(3) Mary
(4) Margaret, widow of William Prestland

| Ann (b.1573) | WILLIAM MORETON III (1574–1654) = Jane Massey dau.of Thomas Lancaster | Mary (1577– after 1648) | Tobias (1578–1648) | Alice (b.1579) | Ellena | Hester (1590?– before 1613) | Jane (b.1596) | Edward (b.1597) | Randolph (b.1598) |

| John (1597–1662) | William (b.1598) | EDWARD MORETON (1599–1674) = Margaret, dau. of William Webb, niece of Archbishop Laud | Peter (1601–58) | Elizabeth (b.1601) | Randolph (b.1602) | Ann (1603–58) | Jane (1606–74) | Philip (1611–69) | Mary (1614–55) |

WILLIAM MORETON IV = (1) Mary, dau. of   Peter (b.1640)   Thomas (b.1641)   Alice   Ann (b.1648)
(1641–1716) | Sir Richard Atkins Bt
Bishop of Kildare and Meath   (2) Mary Harman

Richard   Annabella = William Taylor   Sir WILLIAM MORETON = Jane Lawton   Mary   William = Elizabeth
(d.1774)   Recorder of London, MP   (d.1758)   Pepperrell | Royall
(1696?–1763)   m.1742   (b.1746) | m.1767

REV. RICHARD TAYLOR = Frances, dau. of   Henry Hutton = Elizabeth   Charles Hudson = Harriet
(d.1783) | William Scrase   Royall Pepperrell   (later Palmer) | Pepperrell
took name Moreton   m.1791

Louisa, dau. of William Board (1) = REV. WILLIAM MORETON-MORETON = (2) ELIZABETH (d.1849)   C. J. Abraham = Caroline Palmer
m.1787   (1759–1840)   m.1814

William   Edward   FRANCES ANNABELLA = John   ELIZABETH MORETON   CHARLES THOMAS ABRAHAM
(b.1817, d.s.p.)   (b.1819, d.s.p.)   MORETON   Craigie   (1821–1912)   Bishop of Derby 1919
(1820–92)   m.1842   left Little Moreton to Bishop Abraham   (c.1858–1945)

Decay and restoration

Richard Moreton was a graduate of King's College, Cambridge, Chaplain to the Earl of Peterborough, and Vicar of West Dean near Lewes. On his death in 1783 his son William Moreton-Taylor changed his name to Moreton-Moreton, succeeded to Little Moreton, and was inducted to his father's rectory of West Dean the following year. He continued to live in the south of England and the Cheshire estate was managed by Edward Lowndes of Rode, but correspondence between Lowndes and his master shows that the latter was still keen to purchase land adjoining the estate.

The house and 117 acres were let to Mrs Thorneycroft, who it seems often had to contend with the detrimental effects of high winds. In February 1797 the parlour chimney was blown down and Mrs Thorneycroft was forced to use 'Every endeavour to prevent the rain from doing Damage to the sealings below'. Two years later the Gallery roof lost several slates and a sheet of lead, but the house seems on the whole to have been in sufficiently good repair to withstand such emergencies. In 1801 Lowndes wrote to the Rev. William Moreton-Moreton: 'I am happy to inform you we did not feel the least effects of the very violent Hurricane of wind you felt, the old Mansion remains much the same as when you saw it last excepting little Plaster being fallen from the end of the Gallery.'

William Moreton-Moreton clearly took considerable interest in his family home, and in 1801 commissioned a series of drawings from a Mr Byrom. Little Moreton had by this time become an object of romantic interest to artists. John Sell Cotman made drawings of the house for Britton's *Architectural Antiquities of Great Britain* (1808) when he visited Cheshire in 1806. His drawings of the interior of the Great Hall show that it was arranged as a room of some grandeur, although this impression is somewhat dissipated by the chickens scratching about for food among the oak furniture.

Forty years later, some of the important rooms were used for storage purposes, as appears from a detailed illustrated account of a visit to the house in 1847 by the artist James West. By this time the only inhabited part was to the left of the Hall doorway. The Chapel was used as a coal cellar and store, and the garden was neglected. None the less, West found much to interest him and was deeply impressed by the pervading atmosphere of undisturbed antiquity. He ended his account as follows: 'No gossiping Cicerone has interfered with my wanderings. I had groped and stumbled into every available corner disturbing much ancient dust and alarming many venerable spiders.'

Little Moreton helped to inspire the Black-and-White Revival, which transformed Chester into a thoroughly half-timbered city from the 1850s through the work of local architects like T. M. Penson, John Douglas and T. M. Lockwood. Douglas's pupil Edward Ould was also fascinated by the traditional half-timbered buildings of the north-west. He borrowed many motifs from Little Moreton when designing new country houses in the region, such as Hill Bark on the Wirral and Wightwick Manor in Staffordshire (now also National Trust).

On William Moreton-Moreton's death in 1840, his wife Elizabeth inherited a life interest in Little Moreton. Nine years later she was succeeded by their daughter Annabella Craigie who lived at Pau in the south of France, and was rarely in England. Little Moreton continued to be occupied by tenant farmers and continued to decay gently.

By the time Elizabeth Moreton inherited Little Moreton on the death of her sister Annabella in 1892, the house was clearly in need of essential repair. Like her sister, Miss Moreton did not live permanently at Little Moreton Hall, being a Sister of the Community of St John the Baptist at Clewer in Somerset. She was admitted to the Community in 1853 and used her inheritance to build an orphanage and set

The Great Hall; drawing by John Sell Cotman, 1807

The south wing and gatehouse; etching by John Smith after John Sell Cotman, from Britton's 'Antiquities of Great Britain' (1835)

up an endowment fund. According to the Community's historian, 'The total extent of Sister Elizabeth's generosity will probably never be known, but it may safely be said that without her the Community would have been greatly impoverished, and certainly would not have had such fine buildings.'

Elizabeth Moreton also did much to protect Little Moreton. It was probably she who introduced the metal ties in the Long Gallery and Porch Room to stabilise the south range. She also restored and refurnished the Chapel. In the same year that she inherited Little Moreton she wrote to her second cousin, Charles Thomas Abraham, asking him whether he would agree to become the heir to her Cheshire property.

The young man was not her closest relative but his mother was a life-long friend of hers and she had a deep respect for his father's work as a missionary. There was to be only one condition to the bequest: that Little Moreton was never to be sold.

Charles Thomas Abraham, later to become Suffragan Bishop of Derby, described his visit in a notebook dated 1937:

I remember taking a day off at Lichfield in 1892 to run down and see what she said she had left me, and shall not forget the thrill as I topped the rise after Scholar Green, walking from Kidsgrove Station, and saw the front of the old black and white house in spring sunshine confronting me. It has been in my heart and dreams ever since, but it is odd that I have never even heard of it before – a rather wonderful shock of surprise and joy as I prowled around, then until her death a stranger. Mrs Craigie, her sister, had long neglected it. From that time onward Sister Elizabeth lavished I fancy far more than all the income on its stability and maintenance, rescued, visited and loved every corner.

Bishop Abraham took possession of his inheritance in 1913 and continued the work of preservation initiated by his cousin. He sought the advice of the Society for the Protection of Ancient Buildings, and the Society's leading architect-craftsman, William Weir, who had been William Morris's secretary and Philip Webb's favourite pupil, devoted the rest of his working life to repairing Little Moreton. Bishop Abraham himself rescued the pewter plate from the cellar, and the oak hall table and spice chest mentioned in the 1599 inventory from the kitchen. The octagonal table now in the Withdrawing Room and the Moreton armorial glass were found buried in a heap of plaster. He also opened the house regularly to the public.

In 1937 Bishop Abraham and his son Rupert generously offered the hall and its contents to the National Trust. James Lees-Milne, who handled the negotiations for the Trust, described the bishop as 'a delightful old man with white hair, a soft mouth and slanting lids over eyes that radiated benignity and kindliness … a diffident, unassuming and distinguished cleric of the old school'. The Abrahams' offer was accepted on the understanding that they should be recompensed for the cost of providing alternative accommodation for a resident farmer, and of part of the repairs incurred by them during their ownership. A public appeal was launched for this sum and for an additional £1,000 to complete the work of repair outstanding. In 1938 the hall was handed over to the National Trust. In the same year Bishop Abraham wrote in his notebook:

That I have been enabled after deep interest in the old Hall for twenty-five years … to put its future in the hands of the National Trust, would I am sure have met with Elizabeth Moreton's warmest approval

The inner courtyard in the 1870s

and entire satisfaction. She loved the old house whole-heartedly.

For more than a century no conscious architectural changes have occurred, and since at least the time of Elizabeth Moreton, efforts have been made to conserve the building as it has been found. It has long been recognised as good practice to patch, plate, fill and support the existing fabric, once weakened by old age and decay, rather than replace it with something new. What had been a financial necessity during the impoverished Victorian farmhouse days, became policy in the twentieth century.

Although there were in the 1890s, 1920s and 1950s major phases of such repairs, conservative conservation has in fact been a continual commitment. Parts of the south range, for instance, have now been repaired two or three times, and while timber buildings may move in old age without danger, a time had come when it was no longer sufficient simply to splice and patch at areas of decay.

In 1977, finding the massive stone slates on the south range to be insecure, the National Trust, with help from the Historic Buildings Council (now English Heritage), embarked on a six-phase programme of structural repairs which were completed in March 1992. In many areas this latest work, where components had been weakened by repeated repair, has been more radical, of necessity involving the complete replacementof timbers (which, in keeping with the historic presentation of the building, are no longer blackened). Thorough research has preceded restoration of areas which have had to be remade, such as complex moulded windows, to ensure that the building as a whole keeps faith with the design. The evidence of the alterations and earlier repair efforts are not lost, however, as these are either recorded or stored for future study.

Bishop Abraham, who gave Little Moreton Hall to the National Trust in 1938; drawing by William Rothenstein, 1928

(Opposite) Replaced timbers on the gatehouse

Bibliography

The extensive Moreton family and estate papers are in the British Library (Add. mss 33935–42 and Add. Ch 37035–92) and the Cheshire Record Office (dxx 185).

ANON., 'Country Homes: Little Moreton Hall, Cheshire', *Country Life*, xv, April 1904, pp. 594–604.

BROTHERTON-RATCLIFFE, Elizabeth, 'Some recently discovered tile variations at Little Moreton Hall, Cheshire,' *Journal of the Chester Archaeological Society*, lxv, 1982.

COOK, Olive, *The English Country House and a Way of Life*, Thames & Hudson, 1974.

COWARD, T. A., *Picturesque Cheshire*, Methuen, 1903.

HEAD, Robert, 'Old Moreton Hall and its Past and Present Owners', *Transactions of the Historic Society of Lancashire and Cheshire*, xlvii, 1895, pp. 1–12.

LEES-MILNE, James, *People and Places*, John Murray, 1992, pp. 84–92.

ORMEROD, George, *History of Cheshire*, iii, London, 1819; rev. ed., 1882.

PEARCE, Walter J., 'The glazed windows of Moreton Old Hall, Cheshire', *Journal of the British Society of Master Glass Painters*, 1939–42, pp. 68–75.

SALES, John, 'Unfaithful but Honest', *Country Life*, clxxxiv, 23 August 1990, pp. 48–9.

STELL, C. F., 'Little Moreton Hall', *Report of the summer meeting of the Royal Archaeological Institute at Keele*, 1963, pp. 270–4.

TAYLOR, Henry, 'Old Halls in Lancashire and Cheshire', *Transactions of the Historic Society of Lancashire and Cheshire*, xlvii, 1895, pp. 13–20.

TIPPING, H. Avray, 'Little Moreton Hall, Cheshire', *Country Life*, lxvi, December 1929, pp. 798–808.

Little Moreton Hall from the south-east in 1902; photograph by Francis Frith